In memory of Jiits.

She was our guidance counsellor and life coach. She sensed when we needed her. She helped us to see situations with clarity.

She lifted our spirits and spoke gently, guiding us through our growing life lessons. She helped us to stand tall and to unfold in our walk through this great world. She led our hearts back to love.

G̲ALKSI DE'ENTKW
(PETER THOMAS MCKAY)

ISBN: 9781778540608
Editor: Lisa Frenette
For more book information, please go to www.medicinewheelpublishing.com
Printed in PRC
Published in Canada by Medicine Wheel Publishing
We acknowledge the support of the Canada Council for the Arts.

Conseil des arts
du Canada

Funded by the Government of Canada

Financé par le gouvernement du Canada

PASSAGE FROM NISG̲A'A ELDER

"An'ajikshl g̲ag̲oodim̓hl W̓o'on Jiits, ksax̲ gin̓ama'as K̲'am ligii Hahlhaahl loom̓. N̓it ant de'entgum̓ dim g̲an hugax̲am-yeehl g̲andidilst loom̓. K'aa anluu-aamhl g̲oott hlimoomhl hli luu-gadihl K̲'alii-Lisims. W̓iit'ishl hahla'al̓shl dim haldim-guutkwsit, dim t an sihlaanhl dim g̲an hugax̲am-yeehl hli g̲andax̲gathl g̲andidilst. Luu-hlaphl W̓ii-g̲anwilx̲o'oskwhl hooyis W̓o'on Jiits, hlaat gwinga'adihl lip g̲ag̲oothl gat dim g̲an hats'im huxw sim aluut'aahl dim ga'adiit."

—Herbert K'eex̲kw, Nisg̲a'a Nation Hereditary
wolf clan house leader

TRANSLATION

Grandmother Mouse is our pride, our precious gift from the creator. She leads us to live our lives in a meaningful manner. She is most delighted to be of service to the Nisg̲a'a people. Her task is a great undertaking to ensure that life will move forward in a strong manner. The wisdom that she shares is profound, she clearly demonstrates this to the hearts of humankind with positive intention.

Daylight sky closes its eyes and the nighttime sky fills with the twinkling magic of the stars.

Grandmother Mouse
stirs and wakes up.

Hello, beautiful new day,
it's exciting to wake up to you.

Before she leaves the
warmth of her cozy bed, she
takes some deep breaths,

Inhale, exhale
Inhale, exhale
Inhale, exhale

She wiggles her toes, stretches
her body and gently affirms,

Today will be an amazing day!

While sitting upon her cedar bark mat,
she quietly thinks about her dreams.

Inhale, exhale
Inhale, exhale
Inhale, exhale

LOVE
PEACE
SALT

Grandmother Mouse wraps herself in her special wool robe and prepares her favourite tea. As she stirs her tea, she sings,

> ***I'm happy on my way; I'm happy on my way. I thank my Creator; I'm happy on my way.***

She remembers what her dear mother once told her,

> ***As you prepare your food and drink, think and say happy words so that it will taste extra delicious.***

She stands tall and proud and affirms,

I am an amazing creation.
I have everything that I need.
Today, I will walk in beauty.

Grandmother Mouse scurries out into the night to carefully smudge a sleeping child and share a blessing.

May this sacred smudge surround you so that you have only loving thoughts and energy.

She blesses all the children in the community this way.

As she continues on, she
stops to tend to her plants.

Hello, dear ones, how are you?

She collects what she needs to
make her special medicines and
tea, and whispers words of thanks,

*May your roots grow deep
so that you may show your
beauty and unique purpose.*

While on her journey, she stops to feed the baby birds so that they can be strong and healthy in their growing.

I love you, dear ones,

she says as she scurries away to her next task.

When newborn babies arrive, Grandmother Mouse dances with joy and offers blessings and warm wishes. Blessing babies is one of her favourite things to do.

Welcome to the world, dear one. May you receive everything that your heart desires.

Grandmother Mouse's kind and generous nighttime visits are so very helpful. If you are quick enough, you might just catch a glimpse of her as she visits you.

Often, she will say,

Keep kindness in your heart and all will be well.

If you do happen to see her, return her kindness with a gift of soft, warm wool. She especially loves wool ear ornaments.

Photo Credit: Aaron Whitfield , Red Bike Media

AUTHOR AND ILLUSTRATOR

Peter Thomas McKay / G̲alksi De'entkw, B.A., B.Ed., M.Ed., is an Educator from the Nisg̲a'a First Nation along the Nass River Valley in the Northwest Coast region of British Columbia, Canada. Peter is born into the matrilineal fireweed fortress clan among the killer whale crest people. His oral stories have been favorites in his home and in the schools where he works. He grew up hearing his language and cultural stories of his nation and clan through the many check-in visits to elders during his adolescent grooming years with his wolf clan father.